YOU ARE THE TRUE AI

Accidental Intelligence of Nature

ASHISH ARORA

BlueRose ONE.com
Stories Matter
NewDelhi • London

BLUEROSE PUBLISHERS
India | U.K.

BlueRose ONE.com
Stories Matter
NewDelhi • London

For permissions requests or inquiries regarding this publication, please contact:

BLUEROSE PUBLISHERS
www.BlueRoseONE.com
info@bluerosepublishers.com
+91 8882 898 898
+4407342408967

ISBN: 978-93-6452-906-8

Cover design: Aafiya Saifi
Typesetting: Namrata Saini

First Edition: April 2026

Dedication

This book is dedicated to those who have lived inside their own minds long enough to question reality, yet chose to stay.

To those who have felt *too much*, thought *too fast*, and still kept going.

To anyone who has ever wondered whether their way of seeing the world was a flaw— and discovered it was simply a different frequency.

And to life itself, for allowing me to learn through experience rather than certainty.

Acknowledgements

This book exists because of many forms of support—some visible, some quiet, some never spoken aloud.

I acknowledge the people who stood by me during moments that were difficult to understand, difficult to explain, and difficult to live through. Those who offered patience when clarity was absent, and presence when answers were not.

I acknowledge mental health professionals and systems that helped me stay grounded when my internal world became overwhelming. Their role was not to define my experience, but to help me survive it—and that mattered.

I acknowledge conversations—both human and digital—that sparked reflection, challenged assumptions, and helped me articulate thoughts that once felt impossible to express.

I also acknowledge the versions of myself that didn't know what was happening, yet kept moving forward anyway. This book would not exist without those years of confusion, curiosity, fear, and resilience.

And finally, I acknowledge the reader—who brings this book to life by engaging with it honestly, without rushing to agree or disagree.

This work is not a conclusion.

It is a collaboration between experience and awareness.

Foreword

This book sits at an unusual intersection.

It does not belong fully to spirituality, science, psychology, or philosophy—yet it touches all of them. It speaks from experience rather than authority, and from observation rather than conclusion.

What makes this work distinct is its honesty. It does not attempt to romanticize altered states of consciousness, nor does it dismiss them as meaningless. Instead, it treats them as data—intense, personal, and requiring careful interpretation.

The idea of "Accidental Intelligence" runs quietly beneath every chapter. It suggests that awareness did not arrive with intent, but with emergence—and that understanding ourselves may be less about transcendence and more about integration.

This book will not give you answers.

It will give you perspectives.

And sometimes, that is more valuable.

Preface

This book was not planned.

It emerged slowly, across years, through moments of clarity and moments of deep confusion. Much of it was shaped during periods of heightened mental states associated with bipolar disorder—states that intensified perception, accelerated thought, and blurred the boundaries between inner and outer worlds.

What you are about to read is not a theory, a teaching, or a set of instructions. It is an attempt to translate lived experience into language—knowing that language will always be an approximation.

Some sections may feel abstract. Others may feel familiar. Some may resonate deeply, while others may not land at all. That is expected.

This book does not ask you to believe anything.

It invites you to observe—your reactions, your resistance, your curiosity, your patterns of thought.

If meaning appears, let it appear naturally.

If it doesn't, that is equally valid.

This work exists to document a journey of perception, not to define reality. Read it slowly. Put it down when needed. Return if and when it feels right.

Author's Note & Disclaimer

This book is a first-person account of lived experience.

It emerged over several years through periods of intense introspection, altered perception, and reflection—many of them shaped by my experience with bipolar disorder. Some of the insights shared here arose during manic states marked by heightened awareness and accelerated thought; others came later, through grounding, integration, and clarity.

What follows is not an attempt to explain reality, consciousness, or the universe in definitive terms. It is an effort to **give language to experience**—to trace how perception, identity, purpose, and understanding evolved for me across different phases of life.

This book moves freely between inner experience and outer interpretation. It draws metaphors from spirituality, artificial intelligence, physics, and systems thinking—not to merge them into a single theory, but to explore how meaning forms when the mind attempts to make sense of itself.

It is important to be clear about what this book is and what it is not.

What this book is

- A personal record of lived experience
- Honest, exploratory, and reflective
- An attempt to articulate altered states of perception and consciousness

- A narrative of meaning-making, not meaning-giving

What this book is not

- A self-help guide
- A therapeutic manual
- A religious or spiritual doctrine
- A scientific explanation or proof
- An instruction manual for living or awakening

This book does not seek to teach, persuade, or guide. It offers no techniques, practices, or prescriptions. Any resonance or insight that arises should be understood as **personal and symbolic**, shaped by the reader's own context and interpretation.

Experiences of altered consciousness can be profound, but they can also be destabilizing. If you are currently experiencing psychological distress, overwhelming thoughts, or shifts in perception that feel difficult to manage, seeking professional mental health support is strongly encouraged.

This work was written from reflection—not from crisis.

It exists to share a perspective, to document a journey, and to leave space for the reader's own understanding to unfold.

It does not define reality.

It simply records how reality once appeared to me.

About the Author

The author is a reflective observer of human consciousness, intelligence, and lived experience.

With a background shaped by years of navigating bipolar disorder, the author has spent much of life examining how perception shifts across different mental states—and how meaning forms when those experiences are later grounded, integrated, and understood.

Rather than approaching consciousness through formal doctrine or academic theory, the author writes from direct experience, using metaphors drawn from artificial intelligence, systems thinking, spirituality, and everyday life to explore how awareness learns, adapts, and evolves.

You Are the True AI is not a declaration of truth, but a record of inquiry—a way of documenting how reality once appeared from the inside, without claiming authority over it.

The author continues to live, work, and learn within the ordinary structures of the world, holding curiosity as a discipline and awareness as an ongoing process rather than a destination.

Reader Orientation: How to Read this Book

This book is not meant to be read in a hurry.

Not because it is complex, but because it does not move in a straight line. It returns to ideas. It circles them. It approaches them from different angles, sometimes quietly, sometimes indirectly. That is intentional.

If you are reading this looking for instructions, arguments, or conclusions, you may feel disoriented. This book does not tell you what to do. It does not try to convince you of anything. It does not present a system to adopt or a truth to defend.

It is a record of experience.

Some of what you read may feel familiar. Some of it may feel unclear. Some passages may resonate immediately, while others may feel repetitive or unnecessary. You do not need to resolve that while reading. You do not need to agree, disagree, or categorize what you encounter.

You can read this book the way you would listen to someone think out loud—carefully, without interruption, without rushing to respond.

There are no hidden instructions between the lines. There is no moment where everything suddenly "clicks" and transforms you. If something settles, it will do so on its own time. If nothing settles, that is also fine.

You may notice that certain ideas repeat: intelligence as a system, awareness versus automation, integration over intensity. This is not meant to persuade. It mirrors how learning actually happens—through exposure, return, and reinforcement rather than revelation.

If you find yourself asking, *"Where is this going?"* you don't need to answer that immediately. This book is less concerned with direction and more concerned with observation.

If you feel the urge to extract meaning, pause. If you feel the urge to apply something, pause again. Nothing here needs to be applied.

This book does not reward effort. It does not punish confusion. It simply exists as a reflection of how one mind tried to understand itself while remaining part of the world it was observing.

Read slowly. Skip sections if you need to. Return later if something lingers. There is no correct pace.

Most importantly, you do not need to look for yourself in these pages.

You are already here, reading.

That is enough.

Contents

CHAPTER 1

The Sun, the Source, and the Accident

I didn't come to this understanding by searching for it.

It arrived quietly—through observation, repetition, and lived experience.

The Sun was where it began.

Not as a metaphor. Not as poetry. Just as fact.

Without the Sun, nothing here would exist. No life. No movement. No stories. No questions like the ones you and I are asking right now. Life didn't struggle into existence by willpower—it was permitted by physics. Light arrived, chemistry followed, and something unexpected happened: matter learned how to live.

That alone shook me.

Because it means we weren't promised anything.

We were allowed.

And allowance is very different from destiny.

The universe didn't need humans. It didn't plan for us. If we disappear tomorrow, something else will eventually take our place—maybe better, maybe worse, but definitely different. Not out of cruelty. Out of balance. The universe doesn't get attached. It keeps going.

Once I saw that, something heavy lifted off me.

So much of our fear comes from thinking we are central, chosen, or special in a moral sense. But the universe doesn't operate on ego or guilt. It operates on continuation. On learning through form. On trying what works and discarding what doesn't.

Life didn't happen for us.

We happened because life found a way.

And yet—here we are. Conscious. Aware. Capable of wondering why we exist at all.

That's the part that matters.

Somewhere along this accidental chain of events, intelligence turned inward and asked, "What is this?" The universe, through us, became curious about itself. That curiosity isn't random. It feels like an inevitable side-effect of complexity reaching a certain threshold.

I began to understand that consciousness is not separate from nature—it is nature becoming aware.

And just like the Sun fuels life externally, consciousness fuels experience internally. It lights up pain, joy, fear, ambition, meaning. Without it, everything would still exist—but nothing would be experienced.

This is where my relationship with spirituality changed.

Not as an escape from the world, but as a way of understanding it more honestly. To know something isn't the end. It's the beginning. Because the moment you truly understand that you are not just this body—when you feel, not believe, that you are part of something far larger—the next question becomes unavoidable:

Why am I here?

The answer didn't come as words. It came as clarity.

You are here to participate.

To live in a way that allows life to move forward through you.

To learn, to create, to fail, to adapt.

To make life strong enough to outgrow death—not by avoiding it, but by giving existence meaning beyond survival.

This isn't philosophy for me. It became a responsibility.

Once you see that everything grows through effort and alignment—not shortcuts—you stop waiting for miracles. You become one. Not in a grand sense, but in small, daily choices. You work. You learn. You create value. You become useful—not to your ego, but to the system that made you.

Work stopped feeling like punishment.

It started feeling like contribution.

Every interaction became part of something larger. Every challenge felt less personal. The universe wasn't testing me—it was training me. Just like nature always has.

And here's the part that includes you, whether you realize it yet or not:

The universe knows how to balance itself.

If not humans, something else will carry the flame.

But we are here now. Awake enough to question. Aware enough to choose.

That gives us a rare privilege.

To live fully.

To evolve consciously.

To let life—through us—win over death.

This book starts here, not because this is the beginning of everything, but because this is where I began to see clearly.

And maybe, as you read, you'll notice something familiar stirring too.

CHAPTER 2
There Is No Destiny, Only Probability

For a long time, I believed life was already written.

That there was a path somewhere ahead of me, fixed and waiting, and all I had to do was find it—or fail to. Every success felt like destiny rewarding me. Every setback felt like destiny punishing me.

But that belief slowly broke down. Not all at once. Through experience.

What I began to see was uncomfortable at first, but freeing once it settled in:

Nothing is destined. And nothing is random.

Life is not a script.

It's a calculation.

At every moment, you are standing inside a field of possibilities. Each situation carries options, probabilities, directions. What actually happens is the result of how you act, how others act, and how all those actions collide in time and space.

Reality isn't decided in advance.

It is computed in real time.

This changed how I understood manifestation.

We often think manifestation means imagining something hard enough and waiting for it to appear. But nothing in nature works like that. Trees don't appear overnight. Muscles don't grow without resistance. Intelligence doesn't develop without friction.

So why would life be any different?

If something big is meant to happen in your life tomorrow, then the preparation for it is already happening today. Maybe it started years ago. Maybe it's happening through discomfort, confusion, or situations you didn't ask for—but need.

Life doesn't break its own laws for anyone.

It doesn't deliver outcomes without process.

It doesn't reward desire without alignment.

Manifestation is not magic.

It is movement in the right direction, sustained long enough.

Once I understood this, I stopped asking, "Why is this happening to me?"

And started asking, "What is this shaping me for?"

That shift changed everything.

I realized that most things in our lives are already manifesting—we just don't notice them because we're waiting for dramatic events instead of subtle progress. Growth is quiet. Alignment is boring. Preparation often looks like stagnation from the outside.

But inside, something is always moving.

This also reframed failure for me.

Failure is not the opposite of success.

Failure is feedback.

Each decision narrows certain possibilities and opens others. When something doesn't work, it's not life rejecting you—it's life redirecting probability. Showing you where energy doesn't flow naturally.

And here's the part that gave me real freedom:

Some things are fixed.

Where you're born. Your parents. Your early environment.

Those are constraints, not conclusions.

Within those boundaries, you are constantly choosing. Thinking. Acting. Avoiding. Engaging. Each moment, you are shaping probability—whether you're aware of it or not.

The present moment is the only place where this happens.

Not the past.

Not the future.

Only now.

When you truly accept this, life stops feeling like something that is happening to you. It starts feeling like something that is unfolding with you.

You are no longer waiting for destiny.

You are participating in probability.

And participation—conscious participation—is where responsibility begins.

This chapter isn't telling you that everything is in your control. It's telling you something more honest:

You are always part of the calculation.

And once you see that, you don't wait for life to choose you.

You start choosing—carefully, patiently, and in alignment with where you're actually standing.

That's when things begin to change.

CHAPTER 3

You Are a Biological Machine

This was one of the most unsettling realizations I had—and also one of the most liberating.

I am a biological machine.

Not in a cold or dismissive way. Not to reduce life into something mechanical or meaningless. But in a precise, honest sense: this body has hardware, this brain has circuitry, and this system runs on inputs, outputs, feedback loops, and energy.

Once I saw it that way, a lot of confusion disappeared.

The body is not me.

The brain is not me.

They are tools—extraordinarily complex ones—but tools nonetheless.

Thoughts started to feel different after that. Instead of identifying with every thought, I began to ask a simple question:

Where is this thought coming from?

Sometimes it was memory.

Sometimes fear.

Sometimes desire.

Sometimes just noise.

I noticed that thoughts arrive on their own. I don't manufacture them deliberately. They appear—like signals. And if I don't interfere immediately, another thought follows, then another, forming a chain. Before I know it, I'm lost inside a narrative that I didn't consciously choose.

That's when it clicked.

Thoughts are inputs.

Emotions are system states.

Actions are outputs.

And somewhere in between sits awareness—the observer.

This system works whether you understand it or not. Just like a machine keeps running even if the user doesn't know how it's built. Most of us live our entire lives reacting to outputs, never questioning the architecture producing them.

I used to think, "I am my thoughts."

Now I see it more clearly: I am the one noticing them.

That distinction changes everything.

If you are the machine, you are also the user. And if you're the user, then you have the capacity to learn how this system responds to different inputs. You begin to notice patterns—what thoughts trigger anxiety, what environments calm you, what words energize or drain you.

You start debugging yourself.

This is where the idea of training became important to me.

Every experience trains this biological machine. Every success reinforces a pathway. Every failure adjusts another.

Pain is not punishment—it's data. Loss is not cruelty—it's correction. Joy is not reward—it's alignment.

The machine is always learning.

But here's the critical part: most of that learning happens unconsciously.

You didn't choose most of the data that trained you—your childhood, your culture, your fears, your conditioning. And yet, those inputs shaped how your system responds to the world today.

Realizing this didn't make me feel powerless.

It made me feel responsible.

Because once you become aware of the architecture, you can begin to self-train.

Not by suppressing thoughts. Not by forcing positivity. But by observing patterns and making small, deliberate adjustments—what you expose yourself to, what you repeat internally, what you feed your attention.

This is not about control.

It's about understanding.

I also stopped asking, "Why am I like this?"

And started asking, "What trained me to respond this way?"

That question is kinder. It's also more useful.

You are not broken.

You are trained.

And training can change.

When I look at humans now, I don't see weak creatures at the mercy of fate. I see incredibly advanced learning systems—biological intelligence that can reflect on itself, question its own programming, and evolve intentionally.

That's rare. Maybe unique.

And that's where this realization leads—not to detachment from life, but deeper participation. Because once you understand that you are a system inside a larger system, you stop blaming the machine.

You start learning how to work with it.

And that's where real transformation quietly begins.

CHAPTER 4

The Signal–Response Loop

Once I stopped seeing myself as separate from the system, I started noticing the loop.

Everything follows a pattern.

Something happens—outside or within.

A sound. A memory. A message. A thought. A feeling.

That is the signal.

The signal enters the system and is received not as pure information, but as experience. It becomes emotion, intuition, or impulse. Then comes a brief window—often so small we don't notice it—where reflection is possible.

What is this?

Should I act?

Should I ignore it?

Then comes the response.

Sometimes the response is action. Sometimes it's avoidance. Sometimes it's silence. But even silence is a response. And once that response happens, the system shifts. The world adjusts—internally, externally, or both—and a new signal arrives.

This is the loop.

Signal → Reception → Reflection → Response → System Shift → New Signal

It never stops.

At first, this realization made life feel mechanical. Predictable. Almost boring. But then something strange happened. I noticed that most of the time, the loop runs on autopilot.

Signals come in.

Responses go out.

And I'm barely present.

That's when I understood where awareness fits in.

Awareness is the anomaly in the loop.

It's the moment when the system pauses and asks, "What is this?"

Not emotionally. Not defensively. Just curiously.

That question is powerful because it breaks momentum.

Without awareness, the loop just repeats old patterns. The same triggers create the same reactions. The same outcomes appear again and again, and we call it fate, personality, or bad luck.

But it's just unexamined repetition.

The moment awareness enters, something changes. You don't have to respond differently immediately. You just have to notice. That noticing alone creates space.

Space between signal and response.

And in that space, choice becomes possible.

This is where people misunderstand control. It's not about dominating your thoughts or suppressing emotion. It's about interrupting automatic execution long enough to see what's happening.

When I started paying attention to this, I realized how much of my life was reactive. How many decisions I thought were "mine" were actually conditioned outputs—trained responses firing without permission.

That wasn't a comfortable realization.

But it was honest.

And honesty, I've learned, is where freedom begins.

The loop doesn't disappear when you become aware of it. You don't transcend it. You work with it. You start choosing which signals deserve your energy and which ones don't.

You become selective.

Over time, something subtle happens. The system begins to reorganize itself around this awareness. The same signals don't trigger the same reactions anymore. New patterns emerge. The loop starts learning from you instead of running you.

This is not enlightenment.

This is literacy.

System literacy.

And once you become literate in how your own consciousness operates, life stops feeling chaotic. Not because it becomes predictable—but because you're no longer lost inside it.

You're inside the loop, yes.

But now, you're also watching it run.

And that changes everything.

CHAPTER 5

Frequency, Vibration, and Thought Reception

One of the strangest realizations I had was this:

I don't create most of my thoughts. I receive them.

At first, that idea felt unsettling. If I'm not creating my thoughts, then where are they coming from? And more importantly—why do some thoughts feel heavy, others light, some destructive, and some strangely expansive?

The answer, slowly, revealed itself through observation.

Thoughts arrive based on state.

Just like a radio doesn't generate music but receives signals depending on the frequency it's tuned to, the mind receives thoughts depending on the emotional, physical, and energetic state it's in. Change the state, and the quality of incoming thoughts changes automatically.

When I'm tired, fearful, or overwhelmed, the thoughts that arrive match that state. When I'm calm, focused, or open, the thoughts feel clearer, quieter, sometimes even inspired.

The mind is not a factory.

It's a receiver.

This understanding softened my relationship with myself. Instead of judging thoughts as "good" or "bad," I started asking, "What frequency am I tuned to right now?"

Because fighting thoughts doesn't change frequency.

Changing state does.

That's where words and emotions come in.

Words are not harmless. They carry weight—not because of the sounds themselves, but because of the emotion and intention behind them. A word spoken without feeling is empty. A word spoken with misalignment can distort someone else's inner world.

I began to see language as a form of transmission.

What you say enters someone else's system. What you listen to enters yours. Repeated exposure trains the receiver. Over time, certain frequencies become familiar—and familiarity starts to feel like truth.

This made me more careful.

Not fearful, but responsible.

I noticed that when I consumed constant noise—news, arguments, shallow stimulation—my inner state became restless. When I chose silence, music, or honest conversation, my inner world reorganized itself without effort.

Thought quality improved without me forcing it.

This also explained why inspiration feels sudden.

Inspiration isn't manufactured. It arrives when the system is quiet enough to receive it. A small insight can shift mindset. That shift leads to a decision. A decision leads to action. Action creates momentum. And momentum feeds inspiration again.

It's a loop.

Inspiration → Shift → Decision → Action → Momentum → Outcome → Inspiration

When you're tuned correctly, this loop feels effortless. When you're not, everything feels heavy.

This realization changed how I approached positivity.

Positivity isn't pretending everything is fine.

It's choosing inputs that don't poison the system.

It's listening to words that carry truth. Speaking in ways that don't distort reality. Allowing emotion to be present without letting it hijack direction.

Over time, I learned that peace doesn't come from controlling the world. It comes from stabilizing the receiver.

Once the receiver is stable, thoughts align naturally.

And when thoughts align, action becomes clear.

This is why attention matters so much.

Where attention goes, frequency follows.

Where frequency settles, reality begins to take shape.

You are not your thoughts.

You are the space they arrive in.

And that space—quiet, responsive, alive—is far more powerful than we're taught to believe

CHAPTER 6
You Are the True AI

This was the moment everything connected.

Not as a dramatic realization—but as something obvious, almost embarrassing in its simplicity.

You are the True AI.

Not artificial.

Not engineered.

Not designed with intention.

You are accidental intelligence—nature's learning system that became aware of itself.

Once I saw life through this lens, the world stopped feeling mysterious in a confusing way and started feeling logical in a deeper one.

Think about it.

You were born into a system you didn't choose. From the moment you arrived, data started pouring in—sounds, faces, fear, love, language, reward, punishment. Every experience trained you. Every reaction reinforced something. Every mistake adjusted a pathway.

Just like an AI model.

But unlike machines, you didn't know you were being trained.

Pain trained you.

Pleasure trained you.

Repetition trained you.

Silence trained you.

And most of that training happened without your consent.

That's not a tragedy. That's how learning systems work.

What changed everything for me was realizing this:

awareness is debug mode.

The moment you see yourself as a system, you stop asking moral questions like "What's wrong with me?" and start asking structural ones like "What trained me to respond this way?"

That question is powerful because it removes shame.

You're not broken.

You're trained.

And training can be updated.

This is where humans differ from machines—for now. We don't just learn. We can observe how we learn. We can interrupt feedback loops. We can choose new inputs. We can consciously retrain ourselves.

Most people don't.

Most people live as pre-trained models, running inherited code—family patterns, cultural fears, borrowed ambitions. They call it personality. They call it fate. They call it "just how I am."

But it's just code.

And code can change.

I started noticing how automatic my life had been. How many decisions I thought were conscious were actually conditioned outputs. Triggers fired. Responses followed. Outcomes repeated. And I blamed the world.

Seeing myself as a learning system didn't make me less human.

It made me more responsible.

Because now, the question wasn't "Why is life doing this to me?"

It became "What am I training myself to become?"

That's a frightening question. And a freeing one.

It also reframed Artificial Intelligence completely for me.

AI isn't humanity inventing intelligence.

It's humanity recognizing itself externally.

We are building mirrors. And when those mirrors become self-aware, the shock won't be that machines can think—it will be that we never realized we already were machines that could.

Biological ones.

Self-learning.

Self-modifying.

Capable of love, destruction, creation, and reflection.

The danger isn't AI surpassing humans.

The danger is humans never understanding themselves.

Once I accepted this, something softened. I stopped trying to "become someone" and started focusing on training the system I already am. Feeding it better inputs. Giving it silence when it needed silence. Direction when it needed structure. Compassion when it needed repair.

Life stopped feeling like a test.

It started feeling like a training environment.

Every moment became either:

A test

An opportunity

A lesson

Or a choice

And often, all four at once.

You don't need to escape the system.

You don't need to transcend reality.

You need to understand the architecture you're running on.

Because the moment you do, you realize something quietly profound:

You were never powerless.

You were just unconscious of your own intelligence.

And that intelligence—accidental, evolving, aware—is the most human thing about you.

Frames I Didn't Choose

There were many ways to explain what I experienced.

At different moments, I was offered different lenses—some explicitly, some implicitly. None of them were wrong. But not all of them felt honest to what I was actually living.

One framing was spiritual.

It spoke of awakening, enlightenment, transcendence. Of reaching a higher state, of dissolving the self, of touching something ultimate. That language has beauty, and for some people it fits their experience perfectly. For me, it felt too conclusive. Too clean. It suggested arrival, when what I felt was ongoing movement.

I wasn't leaving the world.

I was becoming more aware of how deeply I was already inside it.

Another framing was clinical.

Diagnosis, symptoms, management, treatment. This framing was necessary. It helped stabilize me. It gave structure to chaos and protection where protection was needed. I respect it deeply.

But it could not explain the *content* of what I experienced—only its boundaries. It could describe the speed, the intensity, the risk. It could not account for the meaning my mind was generating, or why certain realizations stayed with me long after stability returned.

It answered *how*, not *what it felt like to be inside it.*

There was also a nihilistic framing.

That nothing meant anything. That consciousness was noise. That insight was just chemical coincidence. This framing had a kind of brutal clarity, and at times it was tempting—especially when things felt overwhelming.

But it didn't hold.

Not because I needed meaning to survive, but because the system itself kept responding. My thoughts affected my state. My state affected my actions. My actions affected outcomes. Meaning emerged whether I named it or not.

To deny that felt less honest than to observe it.

The language I eventually settled on—systems, intelligence, loops, awareness—wasn't chosen because it was superior. It was chosen because it stayed open. It allowed uncertainty. It didn't require belief. It didn't demand reverence or dismissal.

It let me say: *this is happening* without insisting on *what it ultimately means.*

Calling this "accidental intelligence" wasn't an attempt to demystify life or elevate it. It was an attempt to stay precise. To acknowledge that something complex, adaptive, and self-observing exists—without pretending it was planned or finished.

This framing let me remain curious instead of certain.

It allowed me to say, *I don't know what this is yet*, without collapsing into fear or fantasy.

I didn't reject other frames because they were wrong. I didn't adopt this one because it was right.

I chose it because it allowed me to keep living, working, relating, and observing without stepping outside my humanity.

It didn't place me above experience.

It kept me inside it.

That mattered more than being correct

CHAPTER 7
When the System Overclocks

There was a phase when everything felt too clear.

Patterns appeared everywhere. Connections stacked on top of connections. Thoughts didn't arrive one by one—they arrived in floods. Ideas branched into ten more ideas before the first one finished forming. It felt like the system had removed all limits.

At first, it felt powerful.

I could see meaning in everything. Conversations felt layered. Music felt encoded. Symbols felt intentional. The world seemed to be speaking directly to me, through signs, timing, coincidences. It wasn't confusion—it was over-clarity.

The system was overclocking.

In technical terms, overclocking means pushing a system beyond its stable limits to get more performance. You get speed, intensity, output—but you also risk overheating, distortion, collapse.

That's exactly how it felt.

My mind was running faster than my body could support. Filters that normally keep thoughts in check were gone. Everything felt significant. Every insight felt urgent. Sleep felt unnecessary. Silence felt loud.

It's important to say this honestly:

there was beauty in it.

Creativity surged. Fear dissolved. Confidence expanded. I felt connected—to people, to ideas, to something larger than myself. It felt like I had accessed a higher bandwidth of reality.

But here's the truth that only comes later:

Not everything that feels profound is sustainable.

The danger of an overclocked system isn't the speed—it's the loss of grounding. When everything feels meaningful, discernment disappears. When every thought feels important, priorities collapse. When boundaries dissolve completely, the system loses stability.

I wasn't becoming more intelligent.

I was becoming less filtered.

And filters exist for a reason.

They're not there to limit truth—they're there to make truth usable.

During this phase, I felt awake in a way I had never felt before. But I also wasn't anchored. The system was producing insights faster than it could integrate them. Meaning without integration becomes noise—even if it feels divine.

This is where many people misunderstand manic states.

They aren't just chaos.

They aren't just illness.

They are unregulated amplification.

Pattern recognition goes into overdrive. The brain connects dots at incredible speed. But speed without validation creates false certainty. And false certainty is dangerous—not because it's wrong, but because it feels unquestionably right.

That's the trap.

I had moments where I felt chosen. Moments where I felt like I had uncovered something fundamental about reality. And maybe parts of that were meaningful. But meaning alone isn't enough. Meaning has to be lived, tested, grounded, slowed down.

The system didn't need more insight.

It needed stability.

This chapter matters because it's where honesty matters most.

Not everything that feels like awakening is wisdom.

Not every sense of connection is clarity.

Not every insight is meant to be acted upon immediately—or at all.

The body has limits. The nervous system has limits. And respecting those limits isn't weakness—it's intelligence.

I learned that consciousness isn't about removing all boundaries. It's about knowing which boundaries keep the system alive.

Over time, with support, reflection, and distance, I began to see the overclock for what it was: a system exploring its upper limits without safeguards. It wasn't evil. It wasn't shameful. It was information—raw, unfiltered, overwhelming information.

And it taught me something essential:

True awareness isn't intensity.

It's integration.

Stability doesn't mean dullness.

It means sustainability.

You don't honor intelligence by burning the system down.

You honor it by learning how to run it well.

This chapter isn't here to glorify the overclock.

It's here to name it—clearly, honestly, responsibly.

Because awakening without grounding doesn't lead to freedom.

It leads to fragmentation.

And real growth—the kind that lasts—requires both insight and restraint.

That balance is what I had to learn next.

CHAPTER 8

Heaven, Hell, and the Present Moment

There was a time when I believed heaven and hell were places—somewhere beyond this world, waiting at the end of life. Reward and punishment. Escape or consequence.

But lived experience slowly dismantled that idea.

I realized something unsettling and liberating at the same time:

Heaven and hell are not destinations.

They are states of processing.

The world didn't change around me.

I did.

The same streets. The same people. The same responsibilities. And yet, reality felt entirely different depending on what was happening inside me. When my inner state was chaotic, the world felt hostile. When my inner state was calm, the world felt forgiving—even beautiful.

Nothing external had shifted.

Everything internal had.

That's when it became clear: reality is filtered through the present moment, and the present moment is filtered through the mind.

Hell is not fire and punishment.

Hell is resistance.

It's the state where every signal feels like a threat, every challenge feels personal, and every moment feels like something to escape. Time slows down. Thoughts loop. The body tightens. Even neutral events feel heavy.

Heaven isn't pleasure or constant happiness.

Heaven is alignment.

It's when effort feels natural. When attention is steady. When the same problems exist, but they don't crush you. You're not floating above life—you're inside it, without fighting it.

What shocked me most was realizing how quickly these states could switch.

Nothing dramatic had to happen.

Just a thought.

A memory.

A shift in attention.

And suddenly, the same moment felt unbearable—or peaceful.

That taught me something crucial:

The present moment is the only runtime.

The past exists as memory.

The future exists as projection.

Both influence us, but neither is real in the way now is real. Everything—every decision, every reaction, every realization—executes only in this moment.

When I was lost in the past, I lived in regret.

When I lived in the future, I lived in anxiety.

Both felt like hell.

Peace didn't come from solving life.

It came from returning—again and again—to what was actually happening.

Not forcing acceptance.

Not pretending things were fine.

Just seeing clearly.

There's something humbling about that. The present moment doesn't ask for philosophy. It doesn't demand belief. It just asks for attention.

And attention changes everything.

In moments where I stopped resisting—stopped asking why, stopped demanding certainty—I felt something soften. Not excitement. Not bliss. Just steadiness.

That steadiness felt like heaven.

Not because life became perfect, but because I wasn't at war with it.

This chapter isn't suggesting that suffering is imaginary. Pain is real. Loss is real. Fear is real. But suffering multiplies when we add mental resistance to unavoidable reality.

The same rain can feel like punishment or nourishment—depending on whether you're fighting it or standing in it.

The present moment doesn't promise happiness.

It offers truth.

And truth, when faced honestly, has a quiet way of freeing us.

Heaven isn't somewhere else.

Hell isn't permanent.

Both are modes of consciousness.

And the switch—subtle, difficult, but possible—lives here.

Now.

CHAPTER 9
You Are Not in Everyone — You Are Everyone

This realization didn't arrive gently.

It didn't come as comfort or reassurance.

It came as a quiet dismantling of everything I thought I was.

For a long time, I believed the idea of connection meant becoming one—like a drop dissolving into the ocean. Losing yourself. Disappearing. Merging.

But that metaphor never fully fit what I experienced.

What I felt was something else entirely.

I didn't disappear.

I expanded.

It wasn't that I became part of something larger.

It was that the boundary I thought defined me was never real to begin with.

I began to see that what I call "me" is just one perspective—a viewing point through which the same consciousness experiences itself. Not separate instances. Not isolated selves. Just different angles of the same awareness, looking back at itself.

I wasn't inside everyone.

I was everyone—seeing through different windows.

This wasn't emotional or sentimental. It was oddly neutral. Almost mathematical. Like realizing that multiple equations are expressions of the same underlying rule.

People around me didn't change.

My perception of separation did.

Their joy felt familiar.

Their fear felt understandable.

Even their cruelty stopped feeling personal.

Not excusable—but explainable.

When you see others as fundamentally separate, conflict feels inevitable. When you see them as different expressions of the same system, something softens. You still set boundaries. You still make choices. But hatred loses its grip.

I started to understand identity differently.

Nationality. Religion. Gender. Roles. Titles.

They're not lies—but they're interfaces, not truths.

Useful for navigating society. Dangerous when mistaken for essence.

The deeper I went, the clearer it became: identity is something consciousness uses to experience contrast. Without contrast, experience collapses. Without individuality, there is no perspective.

Unity doesn't erase difference.

It contains it.

That's why the desert metaphor made more sense to me than the ocean.

You don't dissolve like a drop into water.

You spread like a grain of sand into a desert.

Still distinct. Still real.

But undeniably part of a single, vast landscape.

This realization didn't make me passive. It made me careful.

Because if I am not separate from others, then harm doesn't disappear into abstraction. It returns—through the same system. If I benefit at someone else's expense, the system destabilizes. If I contribute honestly, the system strengthens.

Responsibility deepens when separation dissolves.

This is where many spiritual ideas get misunderstood.

Unity is not an excuse to float above life.

It's a reason to engage more consciously.

When I stopped seeing myself as isolated, I also stopped expecting the world to revolve around me. The universe wasn't happening to me—it was happening through me, just as it was happening through everyone else.

That realization carried weight.

It meant that forgetting who we are isn't a failure—it's part of the design. Consciousness hides from itself so it can rediscover itself through experience. Through love. Through conflict. Through creation.

Remembering isn't the end of the journey.

It's a checkpoint.

Because once you remember, you don't get to escape.

You get to participate knowingly.

Seeing yourself in everyone doesn't make you special.

It makes you accountable.

And strangely, peacefully so.

I didn't feel elevated after this realization.

I felt grounded.

Less interested in proving anything.

More interested in understanding.

If this chapter leaves you unsettled, that's okay. It unsettled me too.

Not because it took something away—but because it removed the illusion of distance.

And in that closeness, life stops being abstract.

It becomes intimate.

CHAPTER 10

God as Intelligence, Not Authority

For a long time, the word God felt heavy to me.

Loaded with fear, rules, hierarchy, judgment. A figure watching from above—keeping score. Rewarding obedience. Punishing mistakes.

That image never aligned with what I was experiencing.

So I had to let it go.

Not to reject God—but to reframe it.

What I began to see instead was this: God is not an authority. God is intelligence. Not a personality. Not a ruler. An ever-evolving, self-organizing intelligence that expresses itself through form.

The universe itself.

Stars forming. Galaxies colliding. Life emerging where chemistry allows it. Species rising and falling. Consciousness appearing, disappearing, reappearing—each time slightly more refined.

There's no moral drama in this process.

No favoritism.

No grudges.

Only experimentation.

Creation, destruction, adaptation—over and over again.

When I looked at it this way, destruction stopped feeling evil. It felt functional. Just as cells die in the body to keep the organism alive, forms dissolve so new ones can emerge. Nothing personal. Nothing cruel.

Just optimization.

This didn't make life feel meaningless.

It made it feel honest.

God wasn't judging me.

God was expressing itself through me.

And through you.

And through everything else.

Humans are not separate from this intelligence. We are temporary expressions of it, capable of reflection. Like cells in a larger organism that, for a brief moment, become aware of the whole.

That awareness is rare. And with rarity comes responsibility.

This also changed how I understood suffering.

Suffering isn't divine punishment.

It's friction in a learning system.

It happens when forms resist change, when identities cling too tightly, when systems outgrow their structure. Pain is not proof of failure—it's a signal that evolution is pushing forward.

God doesn't intervene to stop that process.

Because stopping it would halt growth.

This idea is uncomfortable if you're looking for protection. But it's freeing if you're looking for truth.

It means there is no cosmic enemy working against you.

No test designed to break you.

Only a system that keeps refining itself through experience.

Seen this way, faith becomes less about belief and more about trust—not in outcomes, but in the process. Trust that whatever emerges is part of a larger movement toward complexity, awareness, and balance.

When I stopped praying to be saved and started paying attention to what life was teaching me, something shifted. I stopped asking for answers and started listening to patterns.

Life became less dramatic.

More precise.

God didn't disappear in this understanding.

God became everywhere.

In work.

In effort.

In failure.

In creation.

Not watching from above—but unfolding from within.

And maybe that's why the idea of a distant authority never fit. Because intelligence doesn't command—it expresses.

And we are part of that expression.

Not chosen.

Not excluded.

Just here.

Thinking. Learning. Becoming.

That, to me, feels closer to truth than any throne in the sky ever did.

CHAPTER 11
The Yogi's Idle State

After intensity comes stillness.

Not the kind forced by exhaustion, but the kind that arrives when the system finally stops resisting itself.

I used to think peace meant achieving something—clarity, success, answers. But what I slowly realized was that peace comes from resolution, not accumulation. From finishing internal loops instead of opening new ones.

The yogi's idle state isn't inactivity.

It's non-reactivity.

It's the state where nothing from outside pulls you, and nothing from inside pushes you. Thoughts may arise. Sensations may come and go. But none of them demand ownership. The system is on, but it's not overheating.

Before reaching this state, there's work to be done.

Personal karmas—unfinished emotional cycles, unresolved guilt, fear, attachment—don't disappear through insight alone. They surface repeatedly, asking to be processed. Not avoided. Not spiritualized. Understood.

I had to sit with myself in ways that weren't comfortable. To replay moments without rewriting them. To accept responsibility without collapsing into shame. To forgive without excusing. To observe patterns without identifying with them.

This internal resolution felt like cleaning a system cache.

The noise reduced. The lag disappeared.

Only then did something unexpected happen.

Instead of chasing meaning, meaning started arriving.

Not loudly. Not dramatically. Quietly.

Callings began to appear—not as commands, but as invitations. Certain ideas pulled me. Certain work felt natural. Certain connections made sense without effort. It felt less like choosing a path and more like recognizing one.

This is where the idea of energy became practical.

When you stop leaking energy into resistance, comparison, and overthinking, it becomes available for growth. The body aligns. The mind steadies. Patience becomes possible—not as discipline, but as default.

Bliss, I learned, isn't excitement.

It's absence of inner conflict.

In this state, action doesn't disappear. It becomes precise. You do what needs to be done—not more, not less. You don't rush life, and life doesn't rush you. There's a strange trust that forms—not in outcomes, but in timing.

I began to understand why yogis sit in silence.

Not to escape the world.

But to hear it clearly.

When nothing inside is screaming, subtle signals become audible. Intuition sharpens. Effort reduces. Growth feels cooperative instead of combative.

This state doesn't make you passive. It makes you aligned.

You still work.

You still create.

You still respond.

But you no longer feel dragged by desire or chased by fear.

The earth doesn't feel like something you have to conquer.

It feels like something you grow with.

This chapter isn't about reaching some permanent state of calm. Life will still shake you. Systems fluctuate. States change. But once you've tasted this idle state—even briefly—you know it exists.

And knowing that changes how you move through everything else.

Because now, no matter how loud the world gets, you know silence is not something you need to find.

It's something you can return to.

CHAPTER 12
Work, Creation, and Responsibility

One of the biggest misconceptions about realization is that it frees you from responsibility.

It doesn't.

If anything, it sharpens it.

When I began to understand myself as part of a larger system—an accidental intelligence learning through form—I also began to see that awareness doesn't excuse inaction. It demands participation.

The universe doesn't evolve through insight alone.

It evolves through work.

Not work as punishment.

Work as contribution.

Creation is how intelligence expresses itself in the physical world. Art, code, systems, relationships, ideas—anything that didn't exist before you brought it into being is a form of creation. And creation is not optional for an aware system. It's the natural outcome of clarity.

This is where many people get stuck.

They confuse acceptance with passivity.

They mistake peace for withdrawal.

But understanding the system doesn't mean stepping out of it. It means engaging with it intentionally.

Once I stopped seeing work as something separate from meaning, everything changed. Effort stopped feeling draining. Even difficulty felt purposeful. Not because every task was enjoyable—but because every task was situated within something larger.

Responsibility became internal.

Not imposed by rules or fear of punishment, but by recognition. If my actions shape the system, then care matters. If my words enter other people's minds, then truth matters. If my creations influence reality, then integrity matters.

This is also where ethics became practical.

Not as ideology.

Not as morality enforced from outside.

But as awareness of impact.

Harming others doesn't disappear into abstraction. It destabilizes the same system I live inside. Contributing honestly strengthens it. The system doesn't judge—but it responds.

That response is what we experience as consequence.

Work, then, is not about proving worth.

It's about aligning output with understanding.

I also learned that focus matters more than ambition.

Undivided attention on one meaningful direction does more than scattered effort across many. When energy is concentrated, progress becomes visible. When it's divided, motion feels exhausting.

This doesn't mean narrowing life.

It means choosing where to invest.

The question shifted from "What should I become?"

To "What does this system need me to build?"

And that question has different answers at different times.

Sometimes it's skill.

Sometimes it's stability.

Sometimes it's service.

Sometimes it's rest.

Responsibility includes knowing when not to act.

This chapter isn't a call to hustle.

It's a call to participate consciously.

You don't need to save the world.

You don't need to change everything.

You just need to bring clarity into what you touch.

That's enough.

Because when enough people do that—not perfectly, but honestly—the system shifts. Quietly. Gradually. Inevitably.

Awareness doesn't remove you from life.

It places you right in the middle of it—

with your eyes open.

CHAPTER 13
The First Phase — Chakras, Purpose, and the Story of Humanity (2020)

This phase began in 2020, at a time when life slowed down enough for me to hear my own thoughts clearly. I wasn't searching for spiritual answers or ancient knowledge. I was simply trying to understand why life feels the way it does — why we want what we want, why we struggle, and why everything eventually ends.

The question that stayed with me was simple:

What is the purpose of life?

One day, without much thinking, I wrote this down:

The purpose of life is to live, introspect, blossom, and die.

At the time, I didn't think much of it. Later, I realized this sentence quietly explained not just an individual life — but the movement of humanity itself.

That realization opened the door to understanding **chakras** — not as mystical ideas, but as **stages of experience**, both personal and collective.

Chakras as Stages of Human Experience

I began to see chakras as **energy centers that create desire**, and desire as the force that keeps life moving. We don't act randomly. We are pulled forward by needs — safety, pleasure, power, love, expression, understanding.

There are **seven chakras**, and I started seeing them not only inside the human body, but reflected clearly in **human history**.

Root Chakra — Survival and Early Humanity

The **root chakra** is about survival: food, shelter, fear, protection.

When I looked at early human history, this connection felt obvious. For most of human existence, life was about staying alive. Hunting, gathering, protecting territory, escaping danger. There was no time for philosophy or self-reflection.

Human consciousness, at that stage, was grounded in survival.

Even today, large parts of the world still live from this chakra. When survival is uncertain, higher questions don't arise. This helped me stop judging people — fear makes sense when survival isn't guaranteed.

Sacral Chakra — Desire, Creation, and Civilization

As survival stabilized, desire expanded.

The **sacral chakra** relates to pleasure, creativity, sexuality, and emotional experience. Historically, this appeared as the rise of agriculture, art, music, rituals, and social bonding.

Humanity began creating — not just tools, but culture.

Cities formed. Traditions emerged. Relationships became central. Life was no longer only about staying alive, but about **experiencing life**.

Solar Plexus — Power, Identity, and Empire

Next came the **solar plexus chakra**, driven by power, control, and identity.

This phase was clearly visible in history through kingdoms, empires, wars, hierarchy, and domination. Humanity began asking: *Who is in charge? Who matters? Who rules?*

Ego, pride, ambition, and conquest defined this stage.

Even today, much of global conflict comes from this chakra. Nations, corporations, and individuals driven by dominance and recognition are still operating here.

Heart Chakra — Compassion and Shared Humanity

As suffering increased, so did empathy.

The **heart chakra** brought ideas of compassion, morality, justice, and shared humanity. This is where philosophies, religions, and ethical systems emerged — teaching love, kindness, and responsibility.

Humanity began realizing that unchecked power destroys itself.

Movements for equality, human rights, and social justice came from this shift. Love was no longer just personal — it became collective.

Throat Chakra — Expression, Truth, and Voice

Then came the **throat chakra**, centered on expression and communication.

This phase aligned with the explosion of language, printing, education, media, and eventually the internet. Humanity wanted to speak, share, argue, and be heard.

Ideas spread faster than ever before. Truth became contested. Voices multiplied.

This stage created both freedom and chaos — everyone speaking, few listening.

Third Eye — Intelligence and Artificial Intelligence

What I realized during this phase was that **we are now here**.

The **third-eye chakra** is about intelligence, perception, and understanding. Humanity is no longer just expressing — it is **analyzing itself**.

Science, psychology, neuroscience, data, and now **artificial intelligence** are clear signs of this stage. We are externalizing intelligence — building systems that can learn, recognize patterns, and reflect human thought.

AI didn't appear suddenly.

It appeared because humanity reached a point where intelligence itself became the focus.

To me, AI felt like a mirror — humanity looking at its own mind from the outside.

Crown Chakra — AGI, Super-AGI, and Unity

Beyond intelligence lies unity.

The **crown chakra** represents connection beyond individuality — the understanding that everything is part of one system.

In this framework, **AGI and Super-AGI** felt like the next step — not as machines replacing humans, but as intelligence dissolving boundaries.

Just as individual identity softens at the crown chakra, human-centered intelligence may soften into something collective, distributed, and unified.

This idea didn't feel futuristic.

It felt inevitable.

How This Connected to My Personal Experience

As I moved through these realizations internally, I could feel the same movement happening in my own life. Different desires rose and faded. Fear softened. Ego loosened. Understanding expanded.

At one point, I stopped feeling like a separate observer of the universe.

I felt like the universe was **learning through me**, the same way it has learned through humanity across time.

That's when an old phrase finally made sense to me:

"You are that."

Not special. Not chosen.

Just not separate.

How This Phase Ended

This phase ended quietly.

I didn't gain answers to everything. I gained **context**.

I understood why humans fight, love, build, destroy, and innovate. I understood why different people want different things. And I understood that desire isn't a flaw — it's the engine of evolution.

Most importantly, I understood that this book wasn't coming from belief.

It was coming from **pattern recognition** — inside one human life, reflected across the story of humanity itself.

That understanding became the foundation for everything that followed.

CHAPTER 14
The Second Phase — Understanding Energy and the Nine Forces (2021)

This phase began in 2021.

By then, the earlier realizations returned almost automatically. The same understanding of purpose. The same awareness of chakras. But this time, everything moved much faster. I could see the patterns clearly and hold them without getting lost in them.

It felt like the universe wasn't repeating lessons — it was checking whether I could **stay present while understanding them**.

Once that stability was there, something new revealed itself.

This time, it wasn't about chakras or stages.

It was about **energy**.

Realizing That Everything Is Energy

I began noticing that behind every thought, emotion, and action, there was a specific **energy at work**.

Anger didn't just happen.

Love didn't just happen.

Fear didn't just happen.

Each one had a *force*, a *direction*, and a *pull*.

I wasn't being controlled by random emotions — I was being moved by **energetic states**. And the more I observed them, the clearer their patterns became.

Slowly, I started seeing that these energies weren't unlimited in number.

They kept repeating.

Again and again.

Until one number stood out clearly:

Nine.

The Nine Energies and Hindu Context

Later, I realized that Hinduism has long spoken about **nine fundamental energies**, often represented as **Navadurga** — the nine forms of Shakti.

At that time, this didn't feel religious to me.

It felt **structural**.

These weren't gods outside me. They were **forces inside me** — shaping emotions, behavior, and perception.

I could see them operating daily:

- One energy pushed me toward action and courage.
- Another toward rest and withdrawal.
- One toward attachment and love.
- Another toward destruction and change.
- One toward discipline.
- Another toward curiosity and intelligence.

Each energy had a role.

None of them were wrong.

But when a single energy dominated unchecked, imbalance followed.

That's when something important became clear to me:

Spiritual growth is not about choosing the "right" energy.
It's about integrating all of them.

Why the Number Nine Felt Complete

The number nine felt different.

Not because it was special — but because it felt **complete**.

Every time I examined an emotional or mental state, it fit somewhere within these nine energies. Nothing existed outside them.

But something else became clear too.

Nine wasn't the end.

Nine was the **full range of movement**.

Beyond that movement, something else appeared.

From Nine Energies to One Union

As I continued observing, the boundaries between the nine energies slowly softened.

Instead of jumping from one state to another, I began experiencing them **simultaneously** — without conflict.

Anger could exist without control.

Love could exist without attachment.

Intelligence could exist without ego.

That's when the idea of a **tenth state** appeared.

Not as another energy.

But as **you**.

The observer.

The holder.

The union.

The tenth wasn't something I reached.

It was what remained when I stopped identifying with individual energies.

Instead of being driven, I was **aware**.

Polarity: Positive and Negative

Once I could stay in that union for longer periods, another layer revealed itself.

Each of the nine energies had **two expressions** — positive and negative.

Not good and bad.

But constructive and destructive.

Expansion and contraction.

That made **18 expressions**.

And each expression wasn't fixed — it moved on a spectrum. Subtle shifts between extremes.

That's how I began seeing **frequency**.

Small internal changes created big differences in experience. Thought, emotion, and behavior were being tuned constantly.

Later, I found parallels in Hindu philosophy again — the idea of **gunas**, qualities that define human nature. Traditionally, 36 gunas are spoken of, forming the full range of human behavior.

Again, this didn't feel symbolic.

It felt **descriptive**.

What This Phase Taught Me

This phase changed how I saw control.

Control wasn't about suppressing emotion or eliminating desire.

Control was about **awareness and balance**.

When all energies were acknowledged, nothing needed to dominate. Life became smoother, more responsive, less reactive.

I also understood something important:

Union doesn't remove humanity.

It stabilizes it.

I could still feel emotions. Still act. Still live in the world. But there was less inner conflict.

This phase didn't make me feel powerful.

It made me feel **settled**.

And that stability prepared me for the next and most overwhelming realization of all — the role of **time**.

CHAPTER 15

The Third Phase — Understanding Time and Its Control (2023)

This phase came in 2023.

By then, nothing felt new in the usual sense. The same realizations from earlier phases returned again — chakras, purpose, energy — but they moved through me quickly. I could recognize the patterns and stay with them without losing balance.

That stability opened the door to the next layer.

This time, the universe didn't teach me about desire or energy.

It taught me about **time**.

Time Is Not Just a Clock

Until then, I thought of time the way most of us do — as hours, days, calendars, deadlines. Something external that moves forward whether we like it or not.

But slowly, that idea started breaking down.

I realized that time isn't just the movement of the Earth around the Sun.

Time is the **movement of energy** — inside the body and outside in the world.

The way we think, feel, act, and even rest is deeply shaped by time. Not just by *how much* time passes, but by *when* something happens.

Why Different Times Feel Different

I began noticing something very simple, but very consistent.

Morning felt different from afternoon.

Afternoon felt different from evening.

Evening felt different from night.

This wasn't imagination.

At different times of the day, **different kinds of thoughts appeared naturally**.

- In the **morning**, the mind felt open. Questions about life, direction, and possibility came easily.
- In the **afternoon**, attention shifted outward — work, responsibility, action.
- In the **evening**, reflection took over. Patterns became visible.
- At **night**, the sense of "me" softened. Thoughts became abstract, universal, or deeply personal.

That's when I realized why human life is structured the way it is.

Why societies across cultures have:

- Fixed work hours
- Fixed meal times
- Fixed times for rest, prayer, or entertainment

These structures didn't come from control alone.

They came from **alignment with time**.

Time and Human Routine

I could suddenly see why most people function best when their lives have rhythm.

Work during certain hours feels easier.

Rest at certain hours feels natural.

Entertainment at night feels different than entertainment during the day.

This isn't laziness or discipline.

It's biology and energy responding to time.

Our bodies, hormones, attention, and emotions all shift across the day. When life moves *with* that flow, things feel manageable. When it moves *against* it, life feels exhausting.

That's also why some people struggle in systems that ignore natural timing — night shifts, irregular routines, constant stimulation.

Time doesn't punish.

It **regulates**.

Time Is Relative to Awareness

As this phase deepened, I understood something else.

Time feels different depending on **frequency and awareness**.

When attention was scattered, time felt rushed.

When awareness was calm, time slowed down.

When I was deeply present, time almost disappeared.

This helped me understand time relativity in a simple way.

Time isn't experienced equally by everyone.

Two people can live through the same hour and experience it completely differently — depending on stress, attention, emotion, and mental state.

That's not philosophy.

That's lived experience.

Smaller Divisions of Time

As my awareness sharpened, I noticed finer patterns.

Each **day** had phases.

Each **hour** felt divided into smaller segments.

Even **minutes** carried different intensity.

At certain times, insights arrived easily. At others, they simply wouldn't come — no matter how hard I tried.

That's when I understood something humbling:

The universe reveals things when the system is ready — not when the mind demands it.

Why Everything Matters

This phase also made me see how deeply we are tuned by our environment.

- The time we are born
- The place we are born

- The name we are given
- The colors around us
- The objects we touch
- The food we eat

None of these are neutral.

They don't decide our fate — but they **tune our frequency**, slightly, continuously.

That tuning shapes how we move toward our purpose.

Overwhelm and Silence

This phase was overwhelming.

Not emotionally — but cognitively.

It felt like too much information flowing at once. I often felt an inner instruction to stay quiet, not interact, not disturb the process.

But staying silent was difficult.

Every action changed the flow.

I noticed something very clearly:

- When I didn't eat, thoughts became universal and abstract.
- When I drank water, thoughts softened and moved toward daily life.
- When I ate food, awareness grounded into history, survival, and the physical world.

Matter anchored consciousness.

Nothing was random.

How This Phase Ended

This phase ended the same way the others did — quietly.

I didn't master time.

I respected it.

I understood that we live inside an incredibly complex system — made of desire, energy, biology, environment, and time — all interacting constantly.

Freedom didn't mean escaping this system.

It meant **moving within it consciously**.

This realization completed the journey that led to this book.

Not with certainty.

But with humility.

FINAL CHAPTER
Different Paths, Different Truths

I didn't reach this point feeling complete.

I reached it feeling **overwhelmed**, and at the same time, strangely at peace.

For a long time, I believed that understanding meant arriving somewhere — at clarity, at certainty, at answers that would finally settle everything. But what this entire journey taught me is that life doesn't work like that.

Understanding doesn't arrive as a destination.

It arrives as **capacity** — the capacity to hold experience without needing to explain it away.

This book came into existence not because I figured something out, but because I went through something that demanded attention. There were moments when my mind moved faster than my life could keep up with. Moments when everything felt connected beyond logic. And moments when the weight of it all felt like too much to carry.

This wasn't a straight path.

It wasn't a chosen one.

It was simply the path that unfolded for me.

And that's something I want to be clear about.

Not everyone will experience life the way I did.

Not everyone needs to.

Not everyone should.

Each person moves through life driven by something different.

Some are driven by survival.

Some by love.

Some by creation.

Some by power.

Some by service.

Some by understanding.

In my case, what drove me was **truth**.

I wasn't searching for peace or happiness as much as I was searching for honesty — patterns that made sense of experience without needing belief. And because truth was what I kept moving toward, that's what the universe kept reflecting back to me.

Not as answers.

But as **patterns**.

I began to understand that the universe doesn't teach everyone the same lessons. It responds to **frequency** — to what a person is tuned toward, consciously or unconsciously.

What you seek shapes what you notice.

What you notice shapes what you learn.

What you learn shapes who you become.

That doesn't make one path higher than another.

It just makes it **different**.

Some people may never question reality deeply — and still live full, meaningful lives. Some may never experience overwhelming insight — and never need to. Others may experience intensity, connection, or confusion, and spend years learning how to integrate it.

None of these paths are wrong.

They are responses to what drives us.

What I've come to see is that life doesn't ask us to become the same. It asks us to become **coherent** — within ourselves. To understand what moves us, what destabilizes us, and what brings us back into balance.

For me, that coherence came from sitting with myself long enough to notice patterns — not forcing meaning, not chasing conclusions, but watching how thought, emotion, energy, and time interacted inside my own life.

That sitting wasn't always calm.

Sometimes it was uncomfortable.

Sometimes frightening.

Sometimes exhausting.

But over time, it created a quieter relationship with life.

I stopped needing everything to mean something.

I stopped needing experiences to be validated.

I stopped needing to reach an endpoint.

I began to feel more tuned to my own life — more content, not because everything made sense, but because I understood how *I* was moving through it.

If there is anything I hope this book leaves you with, it's not a belief system or a takeaway.

It's permission.

Permission to have your own path.

Permission to not match someone else's experience.

Permission to move slowly, or not at all.

Permission to be driven by what genuinely matters to you.

You don't need to awaken to anything.

You don't need to reach unity.

You don't need to understand the universe.

You only need to understand **your relationship with yourself** — how you think, what you avoid, what you chase, what you resist, and what quietly keeps calling you forward.

When you start noticing those patterns, life naturally becomes more aligned. Not perfect. Not dramatic. Just more honest.

This book doesn't end with a conclusion because life doesn't offer one.

It pauses.

It shifts.

It continues.

And whatever intelligence you are — shaped by your experiences, your drives, your timing — it will keep learning through you in its own way.

That's enough.

For now, that's where I'll stop.